FAMILY TREASURES

FAMILY TREASURES

A GUIDE FOR WRITING YOUR STORY

Teddy L. McIlvain
Contributing Editor: Donna Baumgartner

Graphic designer: Kevin McIlvain
© 2015 Teddy L. McIlvain
All verses are from the Common English Bible unless
otherwise noted.

ISBN-13: 9780692515051
ISBN-10: 0692515054
Library of Congress Control Number: 2015913415
Ted McIlvain, Grapevine, TX

TABLE OF CONTENTS

Our Stories · vii
Your Writing Guide · · · · · · · · · · · · · · · · · · · 1
Starting Your Story · · · · · · · · · · · · · · · · · · · 9
You Shall Write Them · · · · · · · · · · · · · · · · 14
You are a Letter of Christ · · · · · · · · · · · · · 22
Create a Memory Bank · · · · · · · · · · · · · · · 30
Describe Your Childhood Home · · · · · · · · 33
Your Personal Parables · · · · · · · · · · · · · · · 38
Your Wisdom in Proverbs · · · · · · · · · · · · · 48
Your Story in Poetry · · · · · · · · · · · · · · · · · 61
Sing for Joy! · 74
The Writing Journal Journey · · · · · · · · · · · 76
Writing as a Way to Remember · · · · · · · · · · 81

OUR STORIES

My story is important not because it is mine, God knows, but because if I tell it anything like right, the chances are you will recognize that in many ways it is also yours. Maybe nothing is more important than that we keep track, you and I of these stories of who we are and where we have come from and the people we have met along the way because it is precisely through these stories in all their particularity, as I have long believed and often said, that God makes himself known to each of us most powerfully and personally. If this is true, it means that to lose track of our stories is to be profoundly impoverished not only humanly but spiritually.

Originally published in *Telling Secrets*
Frederick Buechner

YOUR WRITING GUIDE

THERE IS SOMETHING highly spiritual—something transcendent—about writing personal words on blank pages. It comes from putting pen to paper, creating a place where your words become stories about you and your relationships with family and friends. Write words to describe casual or happenstance contact with someone whose name you do not know but who gave you inspiration to experience life in a new way. Write the memory down. Record it for you and others to read again. Record it for you and others to be influenced, renewed, and empowered.

Where you write your words is completely up to you, but I encourage you to have a journal or spiral notebook with you for writing while you read *Family Treasures*. Where and how you obtain the tools for this story-writing guided tour is up to you. However, I feel compelled to share a story from a student who attended a *Family Treasures* workshop.

Sharon attended one of the workshops and shared how she chose her journal. She said the bookshelf in her home had a small section of blank journals all placed just out of reach on the top shelf. Well-meaning aunts, grandparents, cousins, and friends had each given one of these journals to her and had gift wrapped it, presented it to her, and told her, "I know you have great stories from your life that should be written down. This is for you to fill with your stories." She told me they had all remained completely empty. Perhaps you have a similar stack of untouched journals to choose your companion for this journey from.

Sharon read the first poem she had ever written to her classmates. It was amazing, and the free verse was impressive. She allowed me the privilege of scanning the pages to see some of her stories. With support from fellow students, she learned to believe in herself and proudly record her memories. Watching her progress from a person who referred to herself as "stuck on stupid" to the confident woman who simply recorded her wonderful stories in her style and wrote without concern for structure, punctuation, and spelling was magical. Her story is truly an inspiration to me, and guess what? I wrote about it in this book and in my personal journal.

I'm trusting that her story will influence my grandchildren in the future.

WHAT YOU CAN EXPECT FROM BIBLE REFERENCE AS YOU READ FAMILY TREASURES

The most prominent literary work in Western society is the Bible. Like every model of collected works, the Bible utilizes literary and stylistic devices to bring the words to life and make them memorable. It will be referenced throughout *Family Treasures*, as my ultimate objective is to enable you to write from the heart and produce content written in your own style.

I have chosen three styles of storytelling found throughout the Bible as guides for this book: *parables*, *proverbs*, and *poetry*. In addition, I present three forms of figurative language as tools to guide your writing: *imagery*, *metaphor*, and *simile*. While you read, you will be encouraged to search out scripture in the Bible and determine whether you are reading a proverb, a parable, or poetry. You will also be challenged to determine the figurative language in the verses you choose. A study Bible will be helpful, but a standard Bible application on your phone or computer will work. I recommend the Common English Bible as a resource to have available as you study and write.

PARABLES

Parables are generally attributed to Jesus in the Gospels but are used in various ancient Hebrew texts as well as in other New Testament books. A parable is a short, symbolic story used to illustrate or teach some truth, religious principle, or moral lesson. It is a speech or observation that delivers a meaning through the use of comparison or parallel thought. You will soon see how using parables in the Bible as a place to start your stories will encourage creative thinking to develop in your writing.

PROVERBS

Proverbs are found in many ancient manuscripts, including the Bible. They are attributed to ancient sages and are based on truths observed in common human interaction. They are short, popular sayings that are often repeated by people in the modern age. Although the Bible attributes the book of Proverbs to King Solomon, the proverbs found in the book are usually of unknown and ancient origin and simply express some commonplace truth or useful thought.

POETRY

Early in Hebrew history, poetry became part of the written literature of the people. Old Testament books written in poetry equal approximately one-third of the total writing. Although each may include a short prose section, the books Job, Psalms, Proverbs, Song of Solomon, and Lamentations are all mostly poetry. Job is noted in many Bible commentaries as not only the greatest poem in the Old Testament but also one of the most significant poems in all of literature.

Poetic elements—such as alliteration and rhyme—that are common in poetry today rarely emerge in Hebrew poetry. Instead, the essential formal characteristic of Hebrew poetry is a construction in which the content of one line is repeated, contrasted, or advanced by the content of the next.

The literary structure of the Bible follows many writing trails. There are certainly more styles than the three I chose to emphasize in *Family Treasures*; however, my objective is to help you begin your writing journey in a meaningful and simplified manner. Consequently the styles you will read deserve some definition so that you can understand the early stages of this book.

IMAGERY

> *Then a great sign appeared in heaven: a*
> *woman clothed with the sun, with the moon*
> *under her feet and a crown of twelve stars on*
> *her head.*
> Revelation 12:1

Imagery is using vivid or figurative language to represent objects, actions, or ideas. Chapter 12 in Revelation contains impressive imagery.

Imagery was a common way of talking for ancient writers, and it clarifies the more perplexing verses of the Bible. Using imagery to understand the wording in the Bible can be the biggest and best key to better appreciating the scriptures. Much like God uses terms for things we do know to describe things we don't know, you can use imagery to help people see your story as a reflection of their own.

METAPHOR

> *But now, Lord, you are our father. We are the*
> *clay, and you are our potter. All of us are the*
> *work of your hand.*
> Isaiah 64:8

In this metaphor, God is compared to a potter who molds clay. God's followers are the clay and are a matter of the design and influence of a creator. This is a figure of speech in which a comparison is made between two seemingly unlike things: God as potter and his people as clay. You can think of a metaphor as a comparison between two or more things using descriptive language. Metaphors serve to make difficult-to-understand ideas or concepts more real, and they also fill written script with vivid descriptions that make the words more vibrant and enjoyable to read.

SIMILE

All human life on the earth is like grass, and all human glory is like a flower in a field.
1 Peter 1:24

A simile is a literary device that makes a contrast between two things using the words "like" or "as." In this scripture, "life is like grass" and "human glory is like a flower in a field." Similes make it easier for readers to envision the ideas of an author, and simile is one of the most common literary devices used in the Bible. Similes often compare something to another thing that is easy to visualize, or similes compare things in such a way that communicates a deeper level of meaning.

In each of these examples of imagery, metaphor, and simile from the Bible, the writers are able to convey colorful pictures and deliver deeper meaning in the points they make. By using these literary devices, you will add depth to your story material and anchor the pictures you paint in words. The examples in *Family Treasures* should give you a good idea of how each style is used in any text and more specifically, how these styles are used in the Bible to enhance parables, proverbs, poetry, portrayals, directives, and foresight.

STARTING YOUR STORY

*Now, after having investigated every-
thing carefully from the beginning, I
have also decided to write a carefully
ordered account for you. I want you to
have confidence in the soundness of the
instruction — you have received*

LUKE 1:3-4

FAMILY TREASURES IS a guide for creating a collec-
tion of personal writings to be shared with your
family and friends. This writing guidebook will
help you recall your memories, reflect on the
importance of the moment, and find the words
to write your story in the family treasures journal. Each writing session is designed to help
you figure out what you want to write about
and the best way to express your feelings about
your experience. Writing tips at the end of each

section are intended to support the writing process and help you focus on the best way to tell your personal stories.

Writers often use questions, or prompts, story frames, charts, or outlines to help them figure out what they want to say. In these writing sessions, you will use writer's tools to help you sort out your experiences and how to share them with friends and family:

Memory Banks: Make a list of your memories, and include people, places, and events from your life that made an impression on you or challenged, comforted, or encouraged you. This list will help you decide what you want to write about.

Reflections: Reflections are written to help you explain why moments should be recorded as a written story for your family and friends. During personal writing times, you will reflect or think about why you believe a finished writing is valuable and inspirational.

Journals: Write about your memories in a notebook. The important pieces of your life will become valuable seeds for your stories. Your journal will be a place for you to try out ideas, play with words, and use the writing process in order to finish a piece that might be read by your family and friends. When they read your words, they will learn more about you, understand your faith journey, and appreciate the writings you leave in your family treasures journal.

I think the best way to explain your faith journey is to write your story like the writings in the scriptures. We learn about life and healthy relationships from the parables of Jesus, the proverbs of Solomon, and the poetry of David. *Family Treasures* is a writing project that uses examples from the scripture to guide you as you plan and write your story so that your family and friends will understand who you are. Expect your words to help build a stronger relationship with present-day readers. Through your written message, future generations of readers will know about the life you are living and understand the beliefs and values you possess and cherish.

I encourage you to spend time in your study Bible exploring the referenced scriptures. Reading Bible verses and studying the story behind the scriptures will help you as you work to find the words you need to best share your story.

Personal Parables: Writing short stories about personal experiences and the lessons you learned help make sense of a situation. Explaining how your faith was strengthened will inspire and encourage your family and friends in their daily lives. Jesus used parables, or short stories, about every day experiences to teach, comfort, and encourage his followers. The parables of Jesus are recorded in the Gospels of the New Testament.

Words of Wisdom: Memories are sometimes exciting and filled with joy, while other important times may be sad or driven by moments of anger. These are the moments of your life. Sharing the words of wisdom that encouraged or comforted you during trying times will be a way for you to pass on wisdom to your friends and family. King Solomon recorded words of wisdom in the book of Proverbs to help people make good decisions and enjoy healthy relationships with others.

Poetry: Writing personal poetry will help your family and friends make connections with your feelings and emotions. The poetry written in your journal will be free verse, like the Psalms. Poetry writing exercises will not dwell on rhyming words but rather on choosing words that describe your feelings. David used figurative language and imagery in the Psalms to reveal deeper feelings and emotions about life and to celebrate the glory of God.

YOU SHALL WRITE THEM

Place these words I'm speaking on your heart and in your very being. Tie them on your hand as a sign. They should be on your forehead as a symbol. Teach them to your children, by talking about them when you are sitting around your house and when you are out and about, when you are lying down and when you are getting up. Write them on your house's doorframes and on your city's gates.

— DEUTERONOMY 11:18–20

AS I PREPARED to write this book and its course curriculum, I asked myself some questions: Why should I leave anything in writing? What could I write that my family and friends would find of value?

One answer came as I remembered preparing for the eminent death of my mother. I was fortunate to have had many years with my parents and felt I knew them well. At the loss of both, I was able to write short poems that summarized my feelings about them. These words were not lengthy, elaborate, or even emotional, but they were simple, written expressions of how I felt about my parents.

Writing about my older brother Von Dearol was much more difficult. When I was a four years old boy, my seventeen-year-old brother died of cancer. When he died, the memories for me passed away with him. Try as I might, I could not find words to write about someone I never knew even though my two remaining brothers and our parents told many stories over the years.

While going through some documents in my mother's personal belongings, I found and read some Bible study notes Von Dearol had written. I saw his report cards and found pictures that revealed parts of his life that I had not known and couldn't possibly remember. Pages in his own handwriting were enlightening and helped me understand something about my brother's life. This discovery of words written in his hand allowed me to realize and finally record my thoughts about a brother I had never known.

Finding clues to an unknown life written on scattered pieces of paper helped me understand the value of leaving personal thoughts and treasures for my family and friends. I realized that it is possible to follow biblical examples and write personal memories as family treasures, which will leave an impact on any reader in the future.

The research for writing this book led me to interesting conversations with people who shared that their parents had left nothing but memories of conversations and moments for them to hold on to in their own life. I invited some of the people I interviewed to attend the first class to tell their stories. I feel it is important to share some of their words with you as you prepare for the writing journey that you will begin with the writing workshops found in *Family Treasures*. The following testimonials from Tom and Sabra help explain the value of writing for friends and families.

TOM'S TESTIMONIAL

Tears streamed down Tom's face as he shared how his father had not told him that he loved him until the day he died. His dad told him,

"Son, I love you. I know I didn't tell you, but I tried to let you know by what I did and not what I said." Then his dad asked him to forgive him. Tom explained nothing was written—no letters, no recordings. There was nothing from his dad but those final spoken words. Then Tom added, "It just wasn't enough. I wish I had something that let me know how my dad felt about his life and his faith. But there is nothing."

So Tom shared his personal story about writing letters to his wife and son. He also described the expressions on their faces when he gave them each a letter in which he had explained how he felt about each of them. Once again, the tears welled up when Tom talked about the letter he was writing to his daughter. He shared how important she had been in his life, and he told us how hard it had been to tell her, "I love you." His next words intrigued me. Tom said, "I want her to know why I love her. How proud I am of her. How I have tried to help her feel protected. How much I want her to know about her daddy and his faith."

Tom's testimony about the importance of written words from family members confirmed my belief that participating in a writing class could be an opportunity to encourage people to describe a life and faith journey to their families for generations to come and, perhaps more importantly, provide written evidence of their feelings.

SABRA'S TESTIMONIAL

Sabra lost the love of her life just over a year before she attended this class. I sat with her as she told me stories about her husband and about the life they had shared together. She sent emails describing how she had gone through his papers and discovered new pieces of memories from her beloved Gordon. The following are her words about her husband, Gordon, and Matthew, their young son who lost his life in a tragic accident, and close family friend Russ. Finding an "empty journal" stuffed with so much love and emotion written on Post-it notes and pieces of scrap paper led Sabra to share her testimony of the importance of finding words from people we love:

THE EMPTY JOURNAL

And the final find...a journal...given to Gordon by Judy and Russ on his birthday 1996...inscribed, "because we believe you have much to say" Nothing is written in the journal...instead there are handwritten papers stuck in between every few pages...all writings of Gordon, most dated and timed in the wee hours of the night... along with a "forward" that says: This is the tattered and torn story of a perfectionist person...and for that reason I am placing handwritten work into the journal rather than trying to actually write in the journal...

There are lists of things like "Positive Influences In My Life" and "Lotto Ticket Dreams" (one of which came to be without a lotto win...the purchase of 2 pieces of property in Montana...but thank goodness we never got the old school bus that was at the top of the list).

One other writing, written some months following Matthew's death, reflects: "I have finally realized that Matthew's death has created an experience that has incredible meaning. In "Praying Our Goodbyes" there is a section about the story of Jesus on the boat in the storm. I interpreted that to mean that one must wake up Jesus in one's life. Matt's death has created that experience (for me) and the next step is to see where this takes me."

One of the last entries is simply titled "Where's Russ," written on the evening of his friend's funeral, a page of musings about where his friend might be, ending with "I'm not really sure, but wherever he is I'll see him again someday…or I will see him tomorrow in the hearts and minds and memories of others"

So, through the tears I must say that this man that I married never ceases to surprise me…even years after he is gone…this time through the writings in an "empty journal."

Sabra Doggett
October 22, 2012

The models for writing our stories and leaving a legacy for our family and friends are found in the scriptures. Friends and family not only enjoy hearing about our personal experiences but also appreciate stories about how life's moments touch our hearts and create memories each day.

Many examples of poems, proverbs, and parables are recorded in the scriptures and preserved for all generations. For example, the apostle

Paul wrote letters to encourage young churches and instruct new Christians and often included examples from his own life. Paul's words teach his readers about the importance of being in communication with God and with each other. Reading the letters from Paul in the New Testament inspire today's Christians to record life moments and spiritual lessons learned from daily living.

Many people worry about their ability to write. Writing our words is more difficult when we stress over structure and rules of our language. Memories of red marks made by English teachers on essays may cause us to hesitate and not write, and that causes us to hide the memories residing in our hearts from our friends and family. As you work through the writing exercises in this book, please ignore any voice that says, "I can't write." Your memories *can* be written down and shared with friends and family. I am convinced that with a little guidance and practice, we can all learn to write and share how we walk with God on life's journey. The words will move easily from our hearts and onto the paper when we think more about what the words mean to us. Tell your story, and don't worry about what an editor might correct.

I believe you will uncover the writer within you.

YOU ARE A LETTER OF CHRIST

*You are our letter, written on our
hearts, known and read by everyone.
You show that you are Christ's letter,
delivered by us. You weren't written with ink but with the Spirit of
the living God. You weren't written
on tablets of stone but on tablets of
human hearts.*

— 2 CORINTHIANS 3:2–3

IN THE NEW Testament, we read letters from the
apostle Paul to the young churches. He sends a
letter of encouragement and comfort for those
who struggle to follow in Christ's footsteps
to Corinth. Everyday struggles of life caused
the people to need reminders of the joys and
rewards of a life as a disciple of Christ. Further, 1
Corinthians 3:2–3 is one of my favorite scriptures

related to what we are doing in this writing class. When you think about what Paul is saying to the church in Corinth, you understand that people see us—our faith, our convictions, and our love for people and life—through the way we live. Scripture suggests that our "writing" is seen in our lives and our actions and not in our perfectly written letters.

IN YOUR JOURNAL

Read the scripture and commentary in your study Bible as you consider Paul's words in 2 Corinthians 3:2–3.

What message is Paul sending in his letter to the new church in Corinth?

How does he compare the Corinthian people to letters?

How does he compare Christians to a letter from Christ?

In what ways does this message encourage Christians today?

Paul also has an urgent message for the Galatians. Paul usually dictated his letters, but in this letter, his message for the church is extremely urgent, and he tells them he is writing with his own hand. He communicates in a unique way and writes in his own hand.

IN YOUR JOURNAL

Read the scripture and commentary in your study Bible as you consider Paul's words in Galatians 6:11–12.

What do the words "large letters...with my own hand" and the exclamation point mean to you? How do we communicate messages of great importance to our family and friends today?

In your journal write your thoughts for these questions:

> What connections could you make between Paul writing letters to people he cared about and your family treasures writing project?
>
> Why is it important to reflect and remember moments in our lives and write down our memories for our family and friends?
>
> Why is your family treasures journal an important writing project?

WRITER'S TIP

A reflection is based on your personal feelings. Just let your ideas move onto the paper to discover a personal purpose for this writing project. Explain why you believe leaving a written account of your life will be valuable and inspirational to your family and friends.

SCRIPTURE AND WRITING

The Bible serves as an inspiration and a model for modern-day Christians to keep a written account of their life and include examples of personal connections to God and their faith. The book of Exodus might be read as a series of journal entries in which Moses describes how the Israelites were led out of Egypt and through the wilderness to Mount Sinai where God reveals himself and offers them a covenant. God's earliest instructions to Moses were to "write all the words of this Instruction on the stones plainly and clearly" (Deuteronomy 27:8).

When the Lord appeared to Moses before the Israelites went into the Promised Land, God said, "So in light of all that, you must write down this poem and teach it to the Israelites. Put it in their mouths so that the poem becomes a witness for me against them" (Deuteronomy 31:19).

"So Moses wrote this poem down that very day, and he taught it to the Israelites" (Deuteronomy 31:22).

There are also many examples of leaving a written account of life for family and friends in the New Testament. Early Jewish disciples recorded the life and teachings of Jesus in the

Gospels of the New Testament, and these early writings continue to encourage Christians today. "Many people have already applied themselves to the task of compiling an account of the events that have been fulfilled among us…I have also decided to write a carefully ordered account for you…I want you to have confidence in the soundness of the instruction you have received" (Luke 1:1–4).

Paul depended on written letters to the new churches to explain and counsel new Christians on the ministry of the church. Paul expresses hope to the ministers of the new covenant in 2 Corinthians 3:3: "You show that you are Christ's letter, delivered by us. You weren't written with ink but with the Spirit of the living God. You weren't written on tablets of stone but on tablets of human hearts."

Prayerfully explore the following scriptures, and see what God reveals to your heart about the importance of leaving a written account of your life. Your thoughts, memories, fears, and dreams as well as a significant history of yourself are treasures for your family and friends.

Read the following scriptures, and write in your journal what you think the verse means and the message you take away from the scripture. How does this scripture prompt you to begin writing down the story of your own life? What is most appealing to you about a family storybook?

Old Testament

Isaiah 8:1-2 (NRSV)
Then the Lord said to me, Take a large tablet and write on it in common characters, "Belonging to Maher-shalal-hash-baz,"and have it attested for me by reliable witnesses, the priest Uriah and Zechariah son of Jeberechiah.

Isaiah 30:8 (NRSV)
Go now, write it before them on a tablet, and inscribe it in a book so that it may be for the time to come as a witness forever.

Jeremiah 30: 1-3 (NRSV)
The word that came to Jeremiah from the Lord: Thus says the Lord, the God of Israel: Write in a book all the words that I have spoken to you. For the days are surely coming, says the Lord, when I will restore the fortunes of my people, Israel and Judah, says the Lord, and I will bring them back to the land that I gave to their ancestors and they shall take possession of it.

Jeremiah 36:1-3 (NRSV) - The Scroll Read in the Temple
In the fourth year of King Jehoiakim son of Josiah of Judah, this word came to Jeremiah from the Lord: Take a scroll and write on it all the words that I have spoken to you against Israel and Judah and all the nations, from the day I spoke to you, from the days of Josiah until today. It may be that when the house of Judah hears of all the disasters that I intend to do to them, all of them may turn from their evil ways, so that I may forgive their iniquity and their sin.

Habakkuk 2:1-3 (NRSV)
I will stand at my watchpost, and station myself on the rampart; I will keep watch to see what he will say to me, and what he will answer concerning my complaint. Then the Lord answered me and said: Write the vision; make it plain on tablets, so that a runner may read it. For there is still a vision for the appointed time; it speaks of the end, and does not lie. If it seems to tarry, wait for it; it will surely come, it will not delay.

New Testament

Luke 1:1-4 (NRSV)
Since many have undertaken to set down an orderly account of the events that have been fulfilled among us just as they were handed on to us by those who from the beginning were eyewitnesses and servants of the word, I too decided, after investigating everything carefully from the very first, to write an orderly account for you, most excellent Theophilus, so that you may know the truth concerning the things about which you have been instructed.

Romans 15:3-4 (NRSV)
For whatever was written in former days was written for our instruction, so that by steadfastness and by the encouragement of the scriptures we might have hope.

Galatians 6:11 (NRSV)
See what large letters I make when I am writing in my own hand!

Hebrews 8:10-11 (NRSV)
This is the covenant that I will make with the house of Israel after those days, says the Lord: I will put my laws in their minds, and write them on their hearts, and I will be their God, and they shall be my people. And they shall not teach one another or say to each other, 'Know the Lord,' for they shall all know me, from the least of them to the greatest.

Revelation 3:7-8 (NRSV)
"And to the angel of the church in Philadelphia write: These are the words of the holy one, the true one, who has the key of David, who opens and no one will shut, who shuts and no one opens: "I know your works. Look, I have set before you an open door, which no one is able to shut. I know that you have but little power, and yet you have kept my word and have not denied my name.

WRITER'S TIP

When you write about a memory in your journal, you have an opportunity to relive an experience and understand the importance of the moment in your life. A reflective journal entry allows you to have a conversation with yourself and see the significance of certain moments in your journey.

As you begin this writing journey, describe what you think the scriptures say about recording your stories and the memories of your life. Explain how you feel and your reactions to that idea. Keep writing until you have a personal understanding of the importance of this writing project.

Writing in your journal allows you to explore ideas, play with words, and plant the seeds of what you will eventually draft and leave as part of your own family treasures journal.

CREATE A MEMORY BANK

Whatever was written in the past was written for our instruction so that we could have hope through endurance and through the encouragement of the scriptures.

— ROMANS 15:4

"SAY CHEESE!" BRINGS a smile to everyone's face just before the photographer snaps the picture. Snapshots capture the event, the people, the places, and the memory of a life moment. Your family treasures journal will include the story behind the picture. Describing life's moments and choosing words to bring the picture to life will help your family and friends understand the value of the memory.

IN YOUR JOURNAL

Writers often make lists or brainstorm ideas about a subject. Making a quick list of words associated with the topic often helps the writer decide where the story will start. Take a minute to travel through the memories in your heart, and jot down ideas about anything you remember. To create a memory bank for your own life in your journal, simply list words and phrases you associate with the following memory moments:

Family	My Childhood
Parents?	Favorite sport?
Siblings?	Fun things you did?
Grandparents?	Unforgettable?
Places I have lived	Friends
Childhood home?	Happiest when?
First home away from home?	Stuff we did?
Favorite room	Reunions?
School Memories	Travels
Favorite teacher/Class?	Favorite place?
Homecoming moments?	Travel experience?
College?	Food memories?

WRITER'S TIP
Now imagine you are looking at a photo album with pictures of all these people and places in your list. Add words that describe the "pictures" and words that tell what you see, what you hear, and how you feel. As you work in your family treasures journal, remember to come back to this page often for writing ideas.

DESCRIBE YOUR CHILDHOOD HOME

*I love the sound of bacon sizzling in
that huge iron skillet that Mama...
I can smell the honey suckle that grew
on the fence outside my window...
The scent of honey suckle and the scent
of bacon—what a wonderful way to
wake up!*

YOUR FAMILY TREASURES might include stories that describe what your life was like as a child. People always enjoy hearing the story that begins with the phrase "when I was your age..." Begin this writing session by thinking about the house you lived in as a child, and capture the memory in your journal.

Think about the house you lived in as a child:

Remember how the house looked from the street and the yard that surrounded it.

Picture entering the house.

Where are the rooms? What things are in the rooms?

Who is in the house with you?

In your journal write:

What does the house look like when you first see it from the street?

What color is the house? What are distinguishing parts of the house?

What is the yard like? Are there trees or bushes?

What do you see from the house if you are standing at the front door?

What do you see when you enter the front door?

What room do you see first? What is in it? What is your favorite piece of furniture in the room? Describe it. What do you like about it?

What room do you want to take a guest to next? What is in that room?

What smells do you remember about the house? What do you want to tell about the smells? Where do they come from? Why are they memorable?

What sounds do you remember about the house? What do you want to tell about the sounds? Where do they come from? Why are they memorable?

What room brings the best memories? Tell about the times in that room.

IN YOUR JOURNAL

Wander back through your answers to the questions. Is there a story you could tell about something you remember from your childhood home? Write your story in your journal. Use sentences that begin with the phrases "What I remember most about my house is…" and "What I loved most was…" Create word pictures, and carefully describe spaces in the home so that your reader can see, smell, hear, and feel your memory. Write in detail about things only you are familiar with, things that you care deeply about, things that may never be known if you don't write about them. You may want to write about a relationship, a family moment, or a more private moment you associate with your childhood home. Write sentences that will help a reader understand why this is an important memory for you. Explain how you feel about this memory, and include the details that will help your reader understand how these moments make your life wonderful, enjoyable, amusing, or troubling.

WRITER'S TIP

Writing about personal memories will stir your heartstrings. *Family Treasures* is designed to help you produce a piece of writing for others to read as a way for your family and friends to understand you and maybe get to know you better. Always keep in mind that you are the one in control of this writing project and the stories you share. As you use your journal to decide what to write about, you may discover that during the writing process, putting certain words on paper will release some feelings and reveal some understanding about a troubling time in your life. You may decide you want to keep these memories private and not reveal certain events of your life publicly. If this happens, you can put your journal aside and write on a separate piece of paper. After the writing is finished, feel free to destroy the paper so that it will never be shared.

People have shown me journals with pages ripped out. One woman told me it felt good to write about a troubling time and then tear the pages out of the journal to destroy them. She shared, "Giving me permission to tear the pages out of my journal gave me relief and satisfaction."

May you find God's blessing in the choices you make.

AUTHOR'S NOTE

Many people worry about their ability to write. It is often difficult to write a story and move words from our heart onto paper if we become too concerned about sentence structures, spelling, or grammar rules. It is my conviction that with a little guidance, we can all learn to write. I believe the writing task will be much easier and words will spill from your heart to your hands and onto a piece of paper when you focus on what the words mean to you instead of how the writing might be graded. Working in a writing journal helps to build confidence as a writer, and sharing your writing with others will be more comfortable. It is my dream that you will write your story as easily as you would tell your story, and as you share what is in your heart, others will get to know you, understand what makes you tick, and appreciate the gifts you leave to them in your family treasures journal.

YOUR PERSONAL PARABLES

People don't light a lamp and then put it in a closet or under a basket. Rather, they place the lamp on a lampstand so that those who enter the house can see the light.

— Luke 11:33

I like this scripture because it emphasizes what I believe to be the purpose of this book, *Family Treasures,* and the importance of writing down your stories. You have so many lights in your life that should not be hidden from future generations or even current family and friends. My prayer for everyone is that your light will shine, your stories will impact your readers, and they will see you and your faith more clearly.

In Matthew 13:35, Jesus says, "*I'll speak in parables; I'll declare what has been hidden since the beginning of the world.*"

The parables of Jesus are unique teaching tools. These are simple stories about daily life and common objects and images, and they are told to help us understand more about Jesus and learn about his kingdom and God's grace. In this chapter, you will study the parables recorded in the Gospels and discover how parables are short stories with a message. Parables from the New Testament will be the inspiration to write a personal parable based on a memory of an event in your life. This personal parable is intended to help your family and friends understand more about you, the world you live in, how your faith was strengthened, and how scriptures helped you understand how to deal with moments in your life.

In the New Testament, Mark records a series of traditional stories about Jesus that have been passed on through oral tradition. He organizes these parables in order to provide a new explanation and experience of Jesus to his audience. In Mark's gospel Jesus is teaching. The people hear the story, but only the disciples understand the message. Often the message is clearest when Jesus tells a parable about an unknown person in an everyday situation. The character is intended to question a common belief of the times that Pharisees and priests were above reproach in the way they lived.

The parables are stories that create pictures about life using words, and Jesus uses everyday objects and situations so that the story is easily understood. But when Jesus includes metaphors and compares things that are not necessarily alike, the parable causes people to pause, think, and unravel the message and increase their understanding of Jesus and his kingdom He teaches very clearly about his adversaries during his ministry on earth and what is expected from his followers.

Composing personal parables allows you to offer an explanation about an experience from your life and provide a better understanding of yourself for your family and friends.

Follow this three-step writing process to compose a personal parable:

1. Search the Gospels, and read the parables of Jesus. The parables are primarily found in Matthew, Mark, and Luke and are often identified by headings in your study Bible. You may select from the following list of some more well-known parables:

PARABLES FROM NATURE

"The Birds of Heaven: Matthew 6:26–27."

"The Flowers of the Field: Matthew 6:28–30."

LOST AND FOUND PARABLES

"The Good Samaritan: Luke 10:25–37."

"The Prodigal Son, or the Loving Father: Luke 15:11–32."

"The Lost Coin: Luke 15:8–10."

"The Lost Sheep: Matthew 18:12–14."

2. Choose one that makes a connection between the Jesus's parable and an event in your life or a story that explains an ordinary moment in your life. Make sure to include the faith lesson you learned. In your journal summarize the parable and explain how this parable connects to your own life.

3. Compose a story in which you are the main character. Use descriptive word pictures to help your reader understand the time, the place, and the situation. Explain the conflict or problem and what exactly

was troubling to you. Just tell a simple story, and include your thoughts and feelings to show your reader how you resolved the issue using your faith.

Follow these steps to write your personal parable:

Read the parable, and write down your personal memory connection to the story.

Brainstorm a list of key words you could include in your personal parable to explain your connection.

Write down what you remember about the moment as a simple story, and include your list of key words in your story.

Explain why you feel this is an important story to pass along to future readers.

For example, I have chosen "The Birds of Heaven" (Matthew. 6:26–27) to illustrate this writing process. These two short verses precede the lengthier "Flowers of the Field" parable from Jesus.

I heard my mother use these words so many times to help me feel better about myself and to remain confident and not worry. The words very simply ask us to pay attention to how God cares for his creatures: "Look at the birds in the sky.

They don't sow seed or harvest grain or gather crops into barns. Yet your heavenly Father feeds them. Aren't you worth much more than they are? Who among you by worrying can add a single moment to your life?" (Matthew 6:26–27).

MY WORD LIST

My thoughts...bad day...inadequate...embarrassed...grades not so good...Coach Griffin...spiteful words from a girl on the bus...crushed...my mother's words...look at the birds...God cares for them...God cares for Teddy...Remember, you are more valuable than the birds.

MY STORY

> *Look at the birds in the sky. They don't sow seed or harvest grain or gather crops into barns. Yet your heavenly Father feeds them. Aren't you worth much more than they are?*
> Matthew 6:26

My mother reminded me of the phrase "Aren't you worth much more than they are?" so many times in my formative years. In the mix of the many days I considered a "bad day," there was a particularly tough one that I remember from high school. It started when I stepped onto the bus that morning. Shirley was what I consider a very proper and socially prestigious person. She looked at me with a disapproving eye and said, "Your Levis are torn on the knee, and look, you have buttoned your shirt out of order." I was crushed, and I placed my hand on my knee to cover that tear—a tear that I had gotten as the result of a proud moment when I slid into second base!

History class added to my "bad day." Coach Griffin was obviously disappointed in our test scores and therefore, he needed to explain how he curved the grades. No names were mentioned as papers were returned discretely, but my grade was the low number on the chalkboard. I was embarrassed, and I quickly covered the number at the top of my test with my hand. It seemed that the whole day was full of nothing but negatives.

When I got off the bus near our farmhouse, I walked straight into my room and cried. As mothers often do, my mother appeared at my door without a sound and asked, "What's wrong?"

I couldn't stop the words and told her everything that had happened. Then, with the words from Jesus that she repeated every time I was worried or feeling bad about myself, she said, "Look at the birds of the air. God loves them and cares for them." And as always, she ended by saying, "Are you not of more value than they?"

WHY I THINK THIS IS IMPORTANT

By human standards, the birds do not seem to plan much farther ahead than their next meal. By our standards, they do nothing about long-term goal setting. I believe this parable is a reminder to me that I am in the presence of a caring and loving God; a God who provides messengers or angels to come to us in times when we do not feel so good. I believe these messengers are led by God's spirit to lift our spirits and comfort us.

Very often during troubling times in my life, parents, siblings, grandparents, and other family members were available to me when I was struggling with a problem. I learned to listen to their concerns and welcomed their hugs. We need to ask God for spiritual guidance. We should always remind loved ones how valuable they are to God and to their family.

The parable about God caring more for me than the birds of the air always reminds me that my mother could comfort me with scriptures and reminders of God's love. From the moment of my firstborn son's birth when I first became a dad, I have held the desire to be a model for my children to see and feel God's love and, in turn, be an example and encourage others.

IN YOUR JOURNAL

Copy the parable and scripture reference for the parable you choose.

Make a list of words that come to mind when you think of the event and circumstances that surround the moment when the parable took on a new meaning for you.

Write your parable as a short story to explain how you worked through a struggle or a challenge in your life. Simply tell what happened and how God's words gave you guidance or strength. Explain how reminders of God's love comforted you.

Connect the importance of the parable to a moment in your life in order to share with your family and friends.

WRITER'S TIP

A personal parable is the writing of a short story that describes an experience from your own life, explains what you learned, and tells how your faith was strengthened. Keep the story short. Focus on the moment, and include details that will help your reader clearly see what is happening and how you feel in that moment. Write to explain how this event strengthened your faith. Let your heart dictate your personal parable and the understanding that is in your heart. Don't be distracted by spelling or punctuation—just focus on sharing this story and your faith with your family and friends.

YOUR WISDOM IN PROVERBS

Don't let loyalty and faithfulness leave you. Bind them on your neck; write them on the tablet of your heart. Then you will find favor and approval in the eyes of God and humanity.

— PROVERBS 3:3–4

PROVERBS IS WRITTEN from the perspective of a wise sage, or a senior person, passing along beliefs, attitudes, values, and wisdom to anyone willing to heed their advice. Reading Proverbs affirms this passing of wisdom to future generations with the introductory phrases "Listen, my children" or "Listen, my son." Proverbs leads me to ask myself several questions: "Where do I get my advice? What sage in my life is offering wisdom and helping me through life? Who will receive my personal wisdom? How can I pass along the life lessons I have learned?"

I recall a person in my life who passed along a life lesson in a remarkable way.

My sister-in-law Ila is a wonderful teacher with an ability to see the best in her students and help them maximize their potential. My brother Bill and I are separated by seventeen years, so I was five years old when I met Ila for the first time. From the very first introduction, she hugged me, talked to me, asked me questions, and made me feel special. I knew she would be an exceptional part of my life, and so she is. Her encouragement and guidance came just when I needed it most, and her words were remarkable and memorable. But I was far from the only recipient of her wisdom.

Recently, she and my brother came to visit my wife and me. As we talked about the trip, she informed me about a student by the name of Azam, who she had taught many years before when he was in the eighth grade at the American Community School (AISK) in Kabul, Afghanistan. He now lived near us, and she wanted to invite him to our house to spend time with her and reconnect during her visit. It had been many years since they had seen each other, but Ila remembered this young man and described him as a brilliant student. His professional career as a physician confirmed that he is a focused and driven man. When he heard that she would be nearby, he was able to join us for an evening of dinner and reminiscing. Azam attributes much of his success to his teacher.

The young physician beamed when he entered our home and embraced Ila and easily recalled past events from their school days. He soon began to share with us memories about his "favorite and most influential teacher" and recalled the proverb she had written on the back of his eighth grade report card. After Azam's eighth grade year at AISK, his father, an Afghan, chose to send him to the United States to live with Azam's brother in Kansas City because of political unrest in Afghanistan. Upon his graduation from one of Kansas City's largest high schools, Azam sent Ila a copy of his valedictory speech "because," he noted, "you have played such a vital part in my life."

"It was simple and so profound!" he said. On the back of his eighth grade report card, she had written, "The best preparation for tomorrow is the right use of today." He said that he immediately recognized the value of her words and took her advice as he began his journey to become both as a research cardiologist and a fine young man. I was captivated by the love, appreciation, and gratitude he expressed to her, and I was in awe of the influence Ila had on his life.

We can relate to the story of the influence this teacher had on her student and recall events in our own lives in which we have been influenced by someone's words. We may even remember times when our words influenced someone else. Whether the words were spoken or written, they were shared, and they remain in the mind and heart of the recipient.

Ila's words of wisdom to Azam are my words of wisdom to you as you participate in this writing workshop. I hope you will remember people who influenced you, and I hope you will write down your story and share it with friends and family. If your stories are not written and shared, your friends and family may miss hearing words of wisdom that inspired change or comforted you. "The best use of today is influencing others tomorrow" are words of wisdom that should inspire you to write down your life story.

Advice from God on preparing for the future is recorded in words of wisdom throughout the book of Proverbs:

Proverbs 6:6–8: "Go to the ant, you lazy person; observe its ways and grow wise.

The ant has no commander, officer, or ruler. Even so, it gets its food in summer; gathers its provisions at harvest."

Proverbs 24:27: "Get your outside work done; make preparations in the field; then you can build your house."

Proverbs 21:31: "A horse is made ready for the day of battle, but victory belongs to the Lord."

Proverbs 27:1: "Don't brag about tomorrow, for you don't know what a day will bring."

As we go back into the scriptures and read biblical proverbs, we are able to glean words of wisdom from scriptures that have been shared from generation to generation. People are able to follow this simple advice from the scriptures and learn solutions to the puzzles of life from ancient sages. Our life improves as we ponder words written three thousand years ago, and when we see how little human nature has changed over all that time, the scripture crosses time and still speaks to us. Wisdom from the Bible helps us understand life, and as we choose to live by

God's word and trust what we read in Proverbs, we store up a wealth of information that can lead us to make better decisions. I am convinced that awareness of scriptures brings about the possibility of behavioral change.

For example, when we read "As iron sharpens iron, so friends sharpen each other's faces" (Proverbs. 27:17), we understand that the phrase "iron sharpens iron" means that in order to sharpen a blade, one must rub an equally strong material against it so that the knife will properly cut and slice. The author uses this metaphor in this proverb to remind us that people attain wisdom by discussing or debating issues and ideas in the fellowship of others. To become wise, we must listen to each other's story and take words of wisdom into our hearts.

Some proverbs require readers to look closely at the particular piece of life the author is examining. Consider Proverbs 13:21: "Trouble pursues sinners, but good things reward the righteous." This proverb looks at the lives of sinners and the lives of the righteous, which are the many people we encounter every day. The words are a reminder that sinners will not only suffer the natural consequences of bad choices, such as injury to their body, to their estate, and to their reputation, but they will also have a guilty conscience and remorse. Guilt is attached to sin and brings punishment with it. The phrase "but good things reward the righteous" reminds us that the righteous shall have the feeling of a good conscience and some peace of mind. Doing things God's way and with understanding and respect brings life and healing to relationships, creates a purpose for this life, and may lead to others being blessed by our lives as well, but the favor of God is the blessing we should seek above all else.

IN YOUR JOURNAL

Several times in the Old Testament scripture, King Solomon offers words of wisdom to help people get along with others. Read and think about the following proverbs in your Bible. In your journal write what you understand about friendship from these words of wisdom:

> Proverbs 17:9: "One who seeks love conceals an offense, but one who repeats it divides friends."

> Proverbs 16:28: "Destructive people produce conflict; gossips alienate close friends."

Proverbs 17:17: "Friends love all the time, and kinsfolk are born for times of trouble."

Proverbs 20:6: "Many people will say that they are loyal, but who can find a reliable person?"

Proverbs 22:11: "Those who love a pure heart—their speech is gracious, and the king is their friend."

Consider the following verses from three translations. Write your understanding about friendship after reading all three:

Proverbs 18:24, Common English Bible: "There are persons for companionship, but then there are friends who are more loyal than family

Proverbs 18:24, New International Version: "One who has unreliable friends soon comes to ruin, but there is a friend who sticks closer than a brother."

Proverbs 18:24, New Living Translation: "There are 'friends' who destroy each other, but a real friend sticks closer than a brother."

IN YOUR JOURNAL

Solomon recorded proverbs as a list of instructions intended to help people make the right decision. It is important to be able to tell right from wrong as we live in our society and develop relationships with our family and friends. As you ponder these proverbs on friendships, write about an experience you had that proved them to be words of wisdom.

The fact that there is an entire book in the Bible titled "Proverbs" leads us to Solomon's writings in the Old Testament; however, authors of the New Testament also include proverbs. Jesus includes proverbs in his conversations with people in the Gospels; Paul shares proverbs in his writings; and proverbs appear in Luke's gospel. Jesus, Paul, and Luke use these words to provide counsel and increase our understanding as we begin to comprehend God's relationship with human creatures as well as our relationships with others. We learn that living wisely is living like Christ and reflects his glory to the world around us.

As you work on your family treasures, the words you use to share events from your life will help your friends and family understand a little more about you. As you record your faith journey and personal feelings about God, your family and friends will understand your personal worth.

IN YOUR JOURNAL

Write what you understand about God's love and reassurance for all people in creation based on the following proverbs found in the New Testament:

Matthew 6:34: "Therefore, stop worrying about tomorrow, because tomorrow will worry about itself. Each day has enough trouble of its own."

Matthew 7:2: "You'll receive the same judgment you give. Whatever you deal out will be dealt out to you."

Matthew 15:14: "They are blind people who are guides to blind people. But if a blind person leads another blind person, they will both fall into a ditch"

Mark 3:25: "And a house torn apart by divisions will collapse."

Mark 6:4: "Prophets are honored every-where except in their own hometowns, among their relatives, and in their own households."

Luke 6:31: "Treat people in the same way that you want them to treat you."

1 Corinthians 9:9: "You will not muzzle the ox when it is threshing."

Galatians 5:9: "A little yeast works through the whole lump of dough."

Galatians 6:7: "A person will harvest what they plant."

IN YOUR BIBLE

Choose a scripture from the Bible that helped you understand how to deal with something in your life. Reflect on the questions below as you choose.

Which proverb often comes to mind when you are making important decisions in your life?

In what ways do Solomon and the first century writers say we should get along with others in the world?

Recall a time when you or a family member used one of the preceding proverbs in conversation.

Recall a time when remembering a proverb might have improved a relationship in your life.

How will writing about an important personal proverb be helpful to friends and family?

IN YOUR JOURNAL

Remember the proverb Ila shared with Azam and how her words guided him to meet his goal of becoming a doctor. Copy a proverb from scripture that helped you understand how to deal with life, and write about what the words mean to you. Think of a specific time in your life when this proverb was particularly helpful to you, and explain how this proverb gave you comfort or encouragement. Describe the moment, and explain to future readers how these words helped you in your life.

WRITER'S TIP

As you reflect on the scripture and its meaning in your life, record your thoughts and feelings. Don't dwell on spelling or punctuation but rather let your ideas flow onto your paper and dictate the story of your life and the feelings in your heart. Keep in mind the purpose of this book is to help you share words of wisdom with friends and family.

YOUR STORY IN POETRY

Do you recognize any of the following expressions?

"Ocean's waves crashing"

"Pinching pennies"

"Taking it over the limit"

"Dipping into the baby's college fund"

"Smelling like a rose"

"Frog-choking rains"

"Worn to a frazzle"

Dropping phrases such as these into your conversations or into your writing is using poetry. Poetry is a specialized use of language to convey figurative rather than literal meaning. Poetry is written to affect our emotions and invites all of our senses to take part in a conversation. Approximately one-third of the Bible is poetry, and the scriptures will be a resource you can appreciate as you study Bible passages and recognize the poetic style of free verse. As you prepare to write poetry for your family treasures journal, be aware of poetry in the scriptures, and determine the difference between poetry and the stories you have been writing in your journals. Poems reach for a strong emotional effect on the reader by using figurative and expressive language.

People often hesitate to sign up for a writing class that offers poetry because of beliefs that haunt them, such as "I can't make words rhyme!" Writing poetry brings on anxiety much like speaking in public or climbing rickety ladders. However, even if you have never written an ode, a limerick, a sonnet, or a haiku, and even if you no idea of various forms of poetry, you must calm your fears. You might discover that you use poetry all the time. People drop descriptive phrases into conversations daily. Remember that poetry uses figurative language to create word pictures to explain what we see and what we feel, has lyrical elements such as repetitive words or contrasting phrases to express personal feelings and may or may not rhyme, and may express strong emotions, such as joy and love or weeping and grief.

As you study the following scriptures and begin writing, search your heart for personal poetry. Play with words, and try writing descriptive expressions you can share with your family and friends that will help them understand how you see certain situations. Examine passages to discover how the imagery, similes, and metaphors charge your emotions and reveal a deeper meaning for your story.

IN YOUR STUDY BIBLE

Colorful language in the Psalms helps the poet explain deep feelings and emotions about a relationship with God. I have chosen figurative language forms—simile, metaphor, and imagery as examples:

Similes compare things using "like" or "as":

Psalm 1:3 "They are like a tree replanted by streams of water."

Metaphors compare things based on a similar quality or attribute they share:

Psalm 23:1 "The Lord is my shepherd."

Imagery paints word pictures by arousing a real sensory experience with people, places, and things:

Psalm 23:2 "He lets me rest in grassy meadows; he leads me to restful waters"

Imagery

He makes me lie down in green pastures.	When I think of this scripture, I allow myself to feel the way I did when I laid in the alfalfa fields on the farm. Cool, wonderful smell, alone...but not alone, confident and at peace. What memories does it bring to your mind?

Open your study Bible to Psalm 1, and as you read this psalm identify similes, and record them in your writer's journal or on the chart. Think about the imagery, and explain how it makes you feel or helps you connect with the topic.

Simile

They are like trees planted by streams of water	*God strengthens people who study, meditate, and obey*

Open your study Bible to Psalm 23. Read, and identify metaphors_in this psalm,_and record them in your writer's journal. Think about the imagery, and explain how it makes you feel or helps you connect with the topic.

You may also find additional imagery in Psalm 23. As you record examples in your writer's journal, think about the imagery, and explain how it makes you feel or helps you connect with the topic.

IN YOUR JOURNAL

Read the following verses, and jot down your thoughts and observations about the images the poet uses. Identify the figurative language such as similes, metaphors, and imagery you find in the scripture.

Song of Praise and Thanksgiving

Shout triumphantly to the Lord, all the earth!
Serve the Lord with celebration!
Come before him with shouts of joy!
Know that the Lord is God—he made us; we belong to him.
We are his people, the sheep of his own pasture.
Enter his gates with thanks; enter his courtyards with praise!
Thank him! Bless his name!
Because the Lord is good, his loyal love lasts forever; his faithfulness lasts
generation after generation.

Psalm 100   Common English Bible (CEB)

Words of Love

You are as beautiful, my dearest, as Tirzah, as lovely as Jerusalem, formidable as
those lofty sights. Turn your eyes away from me, for they overwhelm me!
Your hair is like a flock of goats as they stream down from Gilead. Your teeth
are like a flock of ewes as they come up from the washing pool—all of them
perfectly matched, not one of them lacks its twin.
Like a slice of pomegranate is the curve of your face behind the veil of your hair.
There may be sixty queens and young women beyond counting, but my dove,
my perfect one, is one of a kind.
To her mother she's the only one, radiant to the one who bore her. Young
women see her and declare her fortunate; queens praise her.
Who is this, gazing down like the morning star, beautiful as the full moon,
radiant as the sun, formidable as those lofty sights?

Song of Solomon 6:4-13   Common English Bible (CEB)

Protecting Creation

If I took you to court, Lord, you would win. But I still have questions about your justice. Why do guilty persons enjoy success? Why are evildoers so happy?

You plant them, and they take root; they flourish and bear fruit. You are always on their lips but far from their hearts. Yet you, Lord, you know me. You see me. You can tell that I love you.

How long will the land mourn and the grass in the fields dry up? The animals and birds are swept away due to the evil of those in the land. The people say, "God doesn't see what we're up to!"

If you have raced with people and are worn out, how will you compete with horses? If you fall down in an open field, how will you survive in the forest along the Jordan?

Jeremiah 12   Common English Bible (CEB)

Read the scripture aloud, and listen to the language. Explain the effect of the imagery in the passage and how the words make you feel.

What did you discover about writing poetry from these examples? How can writers take an everyday event and write about it using imagery to draw descriptive word pictures and create poetry? Poetry is more about using words to create feelings and less about using words that rhyme.

Continue to record descriptive phrases from the scriptures. Think about the imagery and emotional effects of the words. Explain the image and how the words help a reader understand the situation. Work until you discover that word choices and phrases, not the rhyming words, evoke emotions and feelings about the experience.

When you consider poems you have read or heard or maybe even memorized in your life, you may remember that you recognize poetry because of the way it sounds and the way it looks on the page. While prose is written in sentences that provide details and explanations of events, poetry is written in lines and phrases like brushstrokes on a canvas to paint a word picture. Whether free verse or rhyming verse, poets work to choose words that will help their reader understand the emotional effect of the situation.

In a clever use of rhyming words and phrasing, the poet Samuel Coleridge leaves us with no doubt that we are in the middle of the ocean and cannot drink the seawater! Recall these lines from Samuel Coleridge's poem "Rime of the Ancient Mariner":

> Water, water everywhere,
> And all the boards did shrink;
> Water, water everywhere,
> Nor any drop to drink.

POETRY WRITING

Look back at your memory moment page in your journal, and think about a situation in your life or an event that you feel very strongly about and the effect of the moment on you.

On a new page in your journal, you can plan a poem about this event by writing this idea in the center of the page and drawing a heart around it.

In the space around the heart, jot down your thoughts that describe the event.

List words or phrases that describe your feelings about the event. Write two or three descriptive word phrases that reveal your thoughts and observations about the events such as:

"I felt as if my heart were floating like a red balloon."

"The sadness sat in my heart like a rock."

"For God alone my soul waits in silence; He is my rock and my salvation and my fortress."

As you explore your thoughts and feelings about events in your life, you may be inspired to write a completed poem to future readers. Read your words aloud, and play with them until they express your emotions. Poetry should be written to be heard.

WRITING TIPS FOR COMPOSING A POEM FOR YOUR FAMILY TREASURES JOURNAL

Find inspiration in your memory bank.

Write a description of the moment. Capture phrases as similes, metaphors, and imagery to explain what happened and reveal how you feel about the moment.

Play with the words until you create a picture for your reader. Think about what you hear, what you see, what you taste, what you smell, and how you feel about the event. Jotting ideas in boxes on a chart might be helpful. (See charts below.)

Include a message in your poem to give your reader something to dwell on after reading your poem. Revise your poem until it is full of descriptive words and phrases that will leave a taste in the reader's mouth. Revise your writing until it expresses your feelings about the moment and guides your reader from reading about the situation to experiencing the situation.

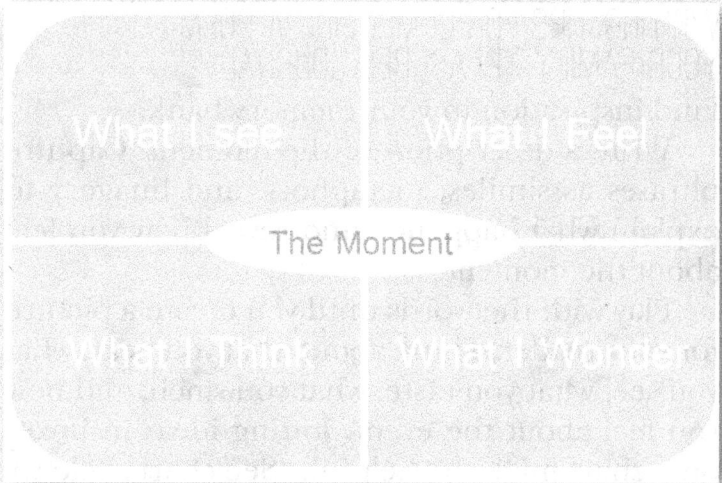

The Moment

| What I see | What I Feel |
| What I Think | What I Wonder |

I participated in this poetry writing exercise in November 2013, five months after our visit to Alaska. The exercise helped me uncover a memory moment when my wife and I landed on a glacier in Denali National Park. I brainstormed using memory boxes, like the template above, and then organized my notes and phrases on a sensory chart, like the one below. As you will see, my poem practically writes itself! As you read my words, you might sense the rise and fall of the small airplane, the cold of the icy glacier on your feet, and the color of the crystal blue ice in the glacier below.

What I see

Bertie's dream to stand on a glacier

Love creating memories with my bride

Aware of the presence of God

Safe in the hands of a confident pilot

Ice and snow chill my feet

Denali - The Tall One' the natives named the mountain

What I feel

Will my grandchildren see this place as I do today?

Can the glaciers be protected?

Will the beauty of God's creation on these mountains be here for others to see?

Will future airplanes dance on the currents to reach this point in the future?

How can we stop the deterioration of the mountain glacier beauty?

Landing on a glacier near Denali

The Moment

What I think

Exhilaration - Anticipation

Warm Sunshine on my face

Anxious to fly

Tiny plane anxiety

Bounced on tires on take off

Bounced on skis on landing

Awe of Denali

Awe of God's creation

Sad my bride is alone two rows back

Happy when she snuggles by my side on the glacier

What I wonder

The mountain - Denali

Sister mountains

Water glistening on the plains

Small Cessna Airplane

White sand snow below

Crystal blue ice patches

Setting sun

Me in the co-pilot seat

My bride 2 rows back

A loving couple separate us

"Landing on a Glacier near Denali in
June 2013"
Oh God, will grandchildren see this place
Where I, in my mother's spirit's presence, on
the glacier stand with
Warm Sunshine on my face.

My bride stands snuggled at my side feeling
Safe in the hands of an unknown bush pilot and
Safer in the hands of God.
Denali, the natives call it.
The tall one is its name.
I, in awe of God's creation,
On this ice field stand.
Will my grandchildren see this place?
Or will God's creatures make it shrink away?
I move like a dancer, the Cessna is my ride
On the currents through the clouds
God's breath does provide.
Anxiety invades my soul, and to my God I pray.
My bride in the fifth seat,
She seems so far away.
The Cessna touches down, and exhilaration
climbs.
Crystal clear and white sands blue the ice below
us now.
The sunshine warms my face.
The snow chills my feet.
And I have to wonder:
Will others see this place?
Or will God's creatures steal its beauty?
Grandchildren not allowed to be where my feet
stand today.

Through the grace of God, I believe they'll
see this place.
Oh God, let it be so.

Ted McIlvain
November 2013

SING FOR JOY!

You've made me happy, Lord, by your acts. I sing with joy because of your handiwork.

— PSALM 92:4

THE EARLIEST POETRY was shared out loud and people chanted, sang, and recited poems to tell a story and express their feelings. David wrote the Psalms to help people see God in their world and worship him. Poetry should be heard!

I would like you to share your poetry with your family and friends and "sing for joy at the works" you have created. Your work may be incomplete, and you may choose to only share a small portion of what will be your finished poem. However, when these bits of poetry are written from your heart they might very well lead to a piece in your *Family treasures* journal that will speak to friends and family in times to come.

Remind yourself of your commitment to tell your story by using this positive affirmation: "I have written from my heart, and I'm proud of my words." Commit to read all or a portion of your poem to someone. You may even want to allow the listener to record their thoughts about your writing in your journal. Ask your listener how the poem makes them feel.

Remember that poems from the heart are written to describe and explain personal experiences.

Relax, and enjoy your accomplishment!

THE WRITING JOURNAL JOURNEY

———— ⌒⌐ ————

FAMILY TREASURES: A Guide for Writing Your Story may have come to an end, but your scripture-inspired writing journey has just begun. You have learned that nothing in your life is ordinary or boring, but it is actually the makings of your life that are meant to be shared with your family and friends in a creative, thoughtful, and loving way. Writing thoughts in a journal has helped you explore your feelings and ideas. Studying scripture and writing in a journal has led you to a new way of thinking about your writing. Use the following exercises to reflect on what you are taking away from this writing experience:

> Think about your writing journey. Write a personal objective that will remind you to continue to put pen to paper and record events, understandings, memories, and dreams of your life. What have you learned about writing in a journal?

Think about your experience with *Family Treasures: A Guide for Writing Your Story*. What impact could your writing have on your family and friends who are blessed to read your words?

Think about what it was like to write candidly and to express openly what you discovered to love about your life. How did you feel when new imaginings about yourself were revealed? How important was combining Bible study and writing exercises?

As you prepare to share your personal writing objective with your family and friends, remember to thank them for their support and encouragement. Decide how to continue to share pieces of your writing with them, and decide if you will just leave your family treasures journal for a reader to discover in the future.

By continuing to open your journal and record your memories and your dreams, you are building a treasured book of personal thoughts and stories. Going forward from this day, give yourself the gift of time to reflect on inspiration from the scriptures and the styles of writing you have learned. Give yourself permission to stop worrying about spelling, punctuation, rhyme, and rhythm. Put thoughts that say you can't write out of your mind. Be assured that what comes from the heart is a window to your soul, which will be discovered by your family and friends in your future writings.

Your inspiration can be found in biblical literature, like the Psalms, and in nonspiritual literature, like the words from one of my favorite authors Rod McKuen. These verses have been an inspiration for me, and I know you will find your own inspiration in your own style and likings.

Psalm 104:24–28: "Lord, you have done so many things! You made them all so wisely! The earth is full of your creations! And then there's the sea, wide and deep, with its countless creatures— living things both small and large. There go the ships on it, and Leviathan, which you made, plays in it! All your creations wait for you to give them their food on time. When you give it to them, they gather it up; when you open your hand, they are filled completely full!"

Excerpts from "I Am Being Led Through Life," a poem in the book *Fields of Wonder* by Rod McKuen:

Fields of wonder
are the places God goes walking,
I found them by mistake and I've trespassed...
To the far fields I have gone,

down along the sea above the hills and back
again thinking I was running new ground all
the time
learning only now that all those wondrous
fields are meadows that a new lifetime would
not last long enough to take me through.

Isaiah 8:1: "The Lord said to me, "Take a large
tablet, and write on it in ordinary letters."

WRITING AS A WAY TO REMEMBER

*Then the Lord said to Moses, "Write
this as a reminder on a scroll and read
it to Joshua."*

— EXODUS 17:14

IN EXODUS GOD tells Moses to write a story as a way
to remember that God was with the Israelites.
In *Family Treasures: A Guide for Writing Your Story,*
memories from your life have emerged in your
personal journal and allowed people who may
not know you to peek into your life and understand you a little better. The author of Exodus
had no way of knowing how the words inscribed
on stone tablets three thousand years ago would
influence future generations. Truthfully, there
is no way of knowing who your words will influence, but if you do not write about your life experiences, future generations might never have a

chance to read your encouraging words and be inspired.

What Moses started in the foundational scripture in the Torah, Paul carried forward in letters to churches familiar with the teaching of Jesus Christ. What God instructed Moses to write in Exodus helped people celebrate God's actions in history, and this led to Paul's letters of instruction to new Christians in the New Testament. These writings bring ideas and scripture forward to us today. In Paul's letter to the church in Rome, he writes, "Whatever was written in the past was written for our instruction so that we could have hope through endurance and through the encouragement of the scriptures" (Romans. 15:4).

It is important to think that writing will be hope for future readers. Moses and Paul set the standard for what is now recorded in your family treasures journal. The prose and poetry you wrote over the past six weeks, journal entries written today and tomorrow, and stories written in the tomorrows to come should be thought of as hope and encouragement for yourself as well as others. Paul continued, "May the God of endurance and encouragement give you the same attitude toward each other, similar to Christ Jesus' attitude. That way you can glorify the God and

Father of our Lord Jesus Christ together with one voice" (Romans 15:5–6).

My prayer for you is that you and your readers will be of one accord and that this writing project might truly glorify God.

Write in peace.